REAL LIFE HEROES
ASYLUM SEEKERS

REAL LIFE HEROES

ASYLUM SEEKERS

Cath Senker

ARCTURUS

This edition first published in 2010 by Arcturus Publishing
Distributed by Black Rabbit Books
P.O. Box 3263
Mankato
Minnesota MN 56002

Printed in China

Series concept: Alex Woolf
Editors: Alex Woolf and Sean Connolly
Picture research: Alex Woolf
Designer: Ian Winton

Library of Congress Cataloging-in-Publication Data

Senker, Cath.
  Asylum seekers / Cath Senker.
      p. cm. -- (Real life heroes)
  Includes bibliographical references and index.
  ISBN 978-1-84837-695-3 (library binding : alk. paper)
 1. Political refugees--Juvenile literature. 2. Forced migration--Juvenile literature. I. Title.
  HV640.S43 2011
  323.6'31--dc22
                        2010014144

Picture Credits
Corbis: cover (Peter Turnley), 7 (Jean Chung), 9 (Reuters), 10 (Ed Kashi), 11 (Michael S Yamashita), 12 (Ali Abbas/epa), 13 (Khaled Al-Hariri/Reuters), 16 (Jacques Langevin/Sygma), 17 (Dmitry Khrupov/epa), 19 (Reuters), 20 (J B Russel/Sygma), 21 (Reuters), 27 (epa), 28 (Pascal Rossignol/Reuters), 29 (Katarina Stoltz/Reuters), 31 (Wendy Stone), 33 (Françoise Demulder), 34 (Rick D'Elia), 37 (Reuters), 39 (Peter Turnley), 41 (Finbarr O'Reilly/Reuters), 43 (Sandy Felsenthal).
Getty Images: 8 (AFP), 14–15 (AFP), 23 (Tom Stoddart Archive/Hulton Archive), 24 (Libor Zavoral/AFP), 25 (Isifa), 35 (Christopher Furlong), 38 (Patrick Kovarik/AFP), 42 (John Moore).

Cover picture: Vietnamese refugees in Hong Kong.

Every attempt has been made to clear copyright. Should there be any inadvertent omission, please apply to the publisher for rectification.

Note from the author
The author would like to thank the following for permission to draw on their material for the stories: Aguek's story: Akol Aguek and Candace Page; Emily and Breyen's story: United Nations in South Africa; Jonathan's story: 'Niños refugiados: Crecer sin raíces' by Luis Miguel Ariza, El País, 04.01.09; Lamara's story: Chechen Republic Ichkeria www.waynakh.com; Muhammad's story: South Eastern Region Migrant Resource Centre, Australia; Samira's story: UNHCR Budapest.

SL001046US
Supplier 03, Date 0510

Contents

Introduction

Which of the following people do you think is an asylum seeker? Soraya and her family, among thousands of others, fled the fighting in Darfur, Sudan, and walked to a refugee camp in Chad. Mina, an Iraqi Christian, left her home in Baghdad for Damascus in Syria, where she applied to go to the United States. Felipe and his family slipped away from their village in Colombia to another part of the country after his father, accused of being a member of a guerrilla group, was attacked by government forces.

Refugees

Mina and Soraya are refugees, but only one of them is an asylum seeker. Refugees leave their country because of conflict or persecution and seek safety in another country. Usually they flee in a crisis, as a large group, and go to the nearest neighboring state.

However, international law provides a narrower definition of refugees. The United Nations (UN) Convention Relating to the Status of Refugees of 1951 defines refugees as people who flee because of a 'well-founded fear of persecution for reasons of race, religion, nationality, membership of a particular social group or political opinion.' It does not include people escaping from war.

Number of new asylum claims, 2008

South Africa	207,000
USA	49,600
France	35,400
Sudan	over 35,000
Canada	34,800
UK	30,500
Italy	30,300

Source: UNHCR — 2008 Global Trends

Only refugees who fit one of the categories in the Convention can claim asylum—the right to seek protection in another country. Soraya, fleeing war, is not an asylum seeker. Neither is Felipe because he has not crossed an international border. He is an internally displaced person (IDP). Mina is therefore the only asylum seeker. She is a Christian, and the Christian minority suffers persecution in Iraq.

Migrants

Most people who move to another country are not refugees. They are migrants who leave to seek a better life in another country. Sometimes, though, the distinctions are not clear. By 2009 around three million Zimbabweans had migrated to South Africa because of the collapse of the economy. Some of them had also suffered

▲ Afghan refugees study Farsi, the Iranian language, at a school run by a non-governmental organization (NGO) in Tehran, Iran. Iran has hosted Afghan refugees for three decades. In January 2009 a total of more than 980,000 refugees were living in Iran.

persecution because they opposed the government of Robert Mugabe. Although not all of them claimed asylum, they left for similar reasons.

Asylum seekers

Asylum seekers, who make an individual asylum claim on the basis of persecution, form a small proportion of refugees. At the end of 2008 there were 15.2 million refugees worldwide. During that year about 839,000 people made individual asylum applications.

Most refugees are in poor countries in the Middle East and Southwest Asia. The greatest number of asylum seekers is in Western Europe, followed by Africa and the Americas. The source countries for asylum seekers vary each year, depending on where the worst conflict and persecution are taking place. Lengthy wars, such as in Afghanistan, Somalia, and Sudan, have caused millions to flee over recent decades.

Real life heroes

Asylum seekers flee their country in desperation. It requires a heroic effort. Typically, they depart quickly, in the midst of danger. There is little time to pack belongings; they may have no passport or travel documents. Refugees pay a high price, both financial and emotional, as they leave their loved ones, their home, job, and possessions. If there is no legal way to migrate, the journey involves huge risks and great uncertainty. They may not know their destination or even if they will arrive alive. Perhaps they will pass through different countries over several years in the search for asylum, living in constant fear of rejection and of being returned to their country of origin.

Some children are forced to flee without their parents. Perhaps their mother and father are dead or died on the journey, or the family became separated during the chaos of flight. Such children may be cared for by other adults en route or left to fend for themselves. Some manage to reach distant countries alone to seek asylum. Most are teenagers but a few are younger. They are known as unaccompanied children.

▲ This boat was carrying African migrants to Tenerife on the Canary Islands, off the northwest coast of Africa. They were rescued by the Spanish coast guard. The Canary Islands belong to Spain, so many migrants attempt to reach the islands as a way to enter Europe. Migrants traveling in this manner risk their lives at sea.

The asylum challenge

Arriving alive at the destination country is just one part of the struggle for survival. Claiming asylum presents another major hurdle. Asylum seekers must make their claim as soon as possible. In some countries they may be locked up in a detention center until their case has been considered. The process can take several years. During this period asylum seekers must put their lives on hold. They are not allowed to work, so they have to survive on welfare benefits or charity, or work illegally.

If their claim fails, asylum seekers are sent back to their country of origin. Some are so fearful of what might happen if they return that instead they go into hiding as "illegals." Successful asylum seekers feel a sense of relief that

Proving persecution

Asylum seekers have to tell their story to government officials to prove they have endured persecution. They are asked to produce documents—for example, to prove which country they come from. Yet in the rush of leaving they may not have managed to bring such paperwork with them. Asylum seekers may be telling the truth about their persecution, but if the officials do not believe the story, the claim can be rejected.

they can remain in a safe country. Now they face the challenge of settling in a new country, while wondering if they will ever be able to return home. Their thoughts will continually be with those they left behind; they anxiously await news from their relatives about the ongoing conflict in their country.

This book tells the stories of some young asylum seekers and their families, the difficulties they have encountered and how they have survived. The stories are all true, but some people's names and aspects of their identity have been changed to protect their privacy.

◀ **These migrants entered Malaysia without the correct documents and are being held as illegal immigrants in a detention camp near the capital, Kuala Lumpur. Many of them are thought to be asylum seekers from Indonesia and Myanmar, countries near Malaysia where the abuse of human rights is widespread.**

Sadil's Story

The Kurdish people

The Kurds come from a region called Kurdistan, which covers parts of Iran, Iraq, and Turkey, and small areas of Syria and Armenia. It is not recognized as a country by the governments of these states. They do not want to give up control of the region to an independent Kurdish state. This has led to conflict, especially between the Iranian, Iraqi, and Turkish governments, and the Kurds. Many Kurds have fled as refugees.

The Kurds of northern Iraq have always wanted to rule their own region. Under Saddam Hussein's rule (1979–2003), the Iraqi government tried to extend its control over the Kurdish area. It carried out brutal attacks on Kurdish villages, sometimes even using chemical weapons. Tens of thousands of Kurds were killed and even greater numbers fled to Iran and Turkey. Kurdish organizations resisted the government and fought for freedom. Sadil is a Kurd from Kirkuk in northern Iraq. His father, Bijar, was active in a political organization that fought for Kurdish rights.

In 2000, when he realized that he was likely to be arrested, Bijar fled Iraq. He departed alone, leaving his wife and three young children aged five, three, and one. Sadil is the middle child. Bijar traveled to Turkey and then to the UK. Bijar successfully claimed asylum and settled in the north of England. He felt safe and he was treated equally to other people.

◀ Kurds in Kirkuk in northern Iraq were removed from their homes by Saddam Hussein's government to make way for Arab Iraqis. Those who refused to leave risked imprisonment and abuse. The Kurds were forced to live in internally displaced people camps, like this one. The photo dates to August 2003, a few months after the US-led invasion of Iraq.

▲ Here, a traditional Kurdish wedding celebration is being held in Jundiyan in northern Iraq. Despite persecution, the Kurds have maintained their language, culture, and customs. They speak Kurdish, wear traditional clothing for cultural events, and celebrate their own festivals, such as Kurdish New Year.

In the meantime, Sadil's mom brought up the children alone. In 2004, when Sadil was seven, the family left Kirkuk. They traveled to Amman, the capital of neighboring Jordan, where they were interviewed at the British embassy in order to obtain visas to enter the UK. This was possible since Sadil's father was already in England. The family then flew to London. Sadil and his little sister didn't recognize their dad when they first saw him.

Bijar brought his family to the north of England. Sadil soon learned English at school. He enjoys many activities that were not available in Iraq, such as going swimming, bowling, and visiting the library. There are some problems. Like most refugees, Sadil's family has been given housing in a rundown area, with problems of vandalism (deliberate damage to property). Sometimes Sadil hears racist comments about "foreigners."

Generally, though, life is better. Sadil feels at home in England and does not want to return to Iraq. Bijar has a job at a cake factory and Sadil's mom is studying English. Yet although the family feels safe, they are concerned for their relatives, most of whom remain in Iraq. They stay in touch by phone. Sadil's family worries constantly that the conflict in Iraq will engulf Kirkuk again.

Mary's Story

Mary comes from Baghdad in Iraq. Life is dangerous there. In 2003 the government of Saddam Hussein was toppled by a US-led international force. Iraqis hoped for freedom, but ever since then there has been conflict. There is fighting between different groups that want power in Iraq, and between Iraqis and the US-led forces that have occupied the country. As a young girl of seven, Mary faced a particularly terrifying danger.

One day a leader of a local gang saw her walking along the street. He thought she was a pretty girl and decided he wanted her as his wife in a couple of years' time. He said she should wear long clothes and the veil when she was out playing, and follow Islamic customs. Her family is not Muslim, though. They are members of a Christian ethnic minority that honors John the Baptist. Things were difficult enough in Baghdad with the continual

▲ A typical scene in Baghdad in 2007 after an anti-government group placed a car bomb in a shopping district in the city center, aiming to kill a police patrol. When the bomb exploded, it killed at least 25 people and wounded more than 50 others.

Iraqi refugees

Since the invasion of Iraq in 2003 and subsequent violence, hundreds of thousands of Iraqis have fled the country. In 2008 the majority—between one and two million people—were living in neighboring Jordan and Syria. These countries have given the refugees access to public services, including health and education. However, most refugees are not allowed to work, so they have to use up their savings or rely on refugee organizations to support them. Although the situation remains highly dangerous in Iraq, some refugees have been forced to return because they ran out of money.

► **An Iraqi refugee waits to receive food rations at a United Nations center in Douma, near Damascus, in 2009. Most Iraqis do not have the right to work in Syria. Many have used up their savings, and the prices of basic goods have risen steeply. Yet the refugees remain reluctant to return to Iraq because of the continuing dangers there.**

conflict and the difficulty of surviving as Christians. This additional threat was the straw that broke the camel's back. Mary's father Mark said they had to leave.

In 2008 Mark paid a taxi driver to take them over the border to Syria. They did not want to stay there, however. There were already over one million Iraqi refugees in Syria, which is a poor country. Many were sheltering in refugee camps, relying on assistance from refugee organizations to survive.

Mary's parents had a tricky decision to make. Her father could have gone to Germany because he has a brother there—it is easier to claim asylum if you already have a connection with the country. But he wouldn't have been able to bring the rest of the family with him. He thought it would be better to go to Sweden, even though he had no connections there. Sweden has a reputation for being generous to asylum seekers. Once refugees have permission to remain, adults can have Swedish language lessons for 18 months and work skills training to prepare them for a job. Children are able to go to school and have special help to learn Swedish. While people are studying and training, they are given money to live on. Most importantly, Sweden allows successful asylum applicants to bring their families.

Asylum seekers in Sweden

Sweden has not taken part in the Iraq war. Yet this Scandinavian country has been welcoming Iraqi refugees since 2003 and hosts more Iraqi refugees than any other Western nation. In 2007 more than 18,500 Iraqis sought refuge in Sweden. Asylum seekers were almost guaranteed to win their asylum claim and were offered generous welfare benefits. In 2008 the Swedish government tightened up the rules to make it harder for asylum seekers to win asylum and began to deport people whose claims had failed.

Mark did not want the whole family to undertake the dangerous trip. Even though conditions in Syria were hard, it was safer for his wife and children to stay there. He would

go first, seek asylum and, once accepted, he would send for them. It was risky for him, and the family would be separated for months or even years, but it seemed like the best plan.

Mark could not go directly to Sweden. His journey involved going by taxi, truck and plane—he even had to make part of the trip on a rubber dinghy. The first European country he came to was Greece. When he eventually arrived in Sweden, he made his way to Sodertalje, south of the capital, Stockholm. In this town there were already more than 7,000 Iraqi refugees, mainly Christians.

On arrival Mark was shocked to find that it was not going to be as easy as he had expected to bring his family to safety. In 2008 the immigration laws in Sweden were tightened up and it became harder to claim asylum. A court ruling found that legally there was no internal conflict in Iraq, which meant that asylum seekers could be sent back to Iraq. Mark's hopes were dashed. In his particular case he was refused asylum because he first arrived in Europe in Greece. He was told that he should have sought asylum there.

Mark is now facing deportation and has to live in hiding from the police. Other Iraqis in his situation have been told to go back to Iraq; some have gone voluntarily while others have been forcibly returned. Any day Mark could be arrested and sent back. He is depressed and feeling hopeless. He cannot get a job because he has no legal status. Now that he has been denied asylum, he cannot get benefits that refugees receive, such as health care, except in an emergency. He is doing his best to avoid being returned to Iraq. The family lives in hope that somehow he will be able to bring them to a safe haven.

◄ **Iraqi refugee children at a school in Sodertalje in 2008. The three students have been in Sweden for less than two years. They learn in a special class for new immigrants where the teacher helps them adjust to Swedish society. The majority of the 16 children in this class are Iraqi refugees. After Swedish asylum rules changed, some Iraqi schoolchildren and their families were deported back to Iraq.**

Fareiba's Story

Afghanistan has suffered conflict for decades. In 1979 the Soviet Union invaded the country, which led to a long civil war. During the 1980s around six million Afghans fled as refugees—about one-third of the total population. The Soviet forces departed in 1989 but the civil war between rival groups carried on. In 1996 an extreme Islamic movement called the Taliban seized the capital, Kabul. In 2001 a US-led force defeated the Taliban and occupied Afghanistan. Fareiba's family escaped when the Taliban still ruled Afghanistan.

Fareiba's family comes from Kabul. The family endured the terrifying civil war of the 1990s. There were continual rocket attacks, and the city was devastated. After the Taliban took power, women were not allowed to go out to work, and girls were forbidden to go to school.

▲ These teenage girls in Herat, Afghanistan, leave their English teacher's home after attending a secret class in 2001. Although the Taliban banned education for girls, some Afghan women organized underground schools in their homes. They risked severe punishments if caught.

▶ A young Afghan woman holds her daughter in a refugee camp on the Tajik–Afghan border, in October 2001. About 3,000 refugees found shelter in this camp. They fled when they realized there would soon be war between US-led forces and the Taliban. At the same time, large numbers of Afghans escaped to Pakistan. The Pakistani government closed the border to prevent more people from entering as refugees.

Fareiba had to stay home. She lived in a large house with her extended family, so at least she had her cousins to play with. However, in 2001, when Fareiba was nine, the Taliban threatened her father, so her parents decided they had to run.

There was no possible legal escape route. The family had no passports, and since Fareiba's dad was wanted by the Taliban, they could not leave openly. They had to pay people smugglers to organize their passage. First they went to Tajikistan. From there they secretly boarded a train to Russia. They had to keep quiet for the entire journey. They were hungry, thirsty, and wanted to use the toilet but they just had to sit quietly.

Women in Afghanistan

Under Taliban rule, women were not allowed to work outside the home; girls were not permitted to attend school or university. When they went out, they were forced to wear a burka, a garment that covers the whole body. After the fall of the Taliban, these rules were overturned. However, after three years of foreign occupation, Taliban forces regrouped to fight the US-led coalition forces and the Afghan government, which was allied to the coalition. As well as war, Afghanistan suffered severe economic problems owing to the failure to rebuild the country after years of devastation. These problems made it hard for women and girls to work and study freely.

From Russia they took a treacherous overland route with other Afghans, using trains and buses. Sometimes they had to walk for tens of miles through the snow. Adults took it in turn to carry the small children on their shoulders, and they ate packets of nuts to give them energy.

They journeyed all the way across Europe to France, where they hid in the back of a truck to go to England. The driver did not know they were hiding, so the people smugglers told them to bang on the side of the truck and scream when they arrived so that he would let them out. They did as they were told. The driver was terrified. He let them out and they ran off down the highway. The police were called and took them to the immigration office, where they were able to claim asylum.

It was very unnerving for the family as they waited for their asylum claim to be processed. They were relieved to find out they had been successful. Fareiba went to school for the first time. She found it hard at first because she knew no English, but she proved to be a fast learner. Fareiba felt safe in the UK and she felt free. It was a big contrast with Afghanistan, where she rarely left the house and could not attend school or even go shopping. The family has integrated well in the community but has kept Afghan customs too. They always cook Afghan food and they celebrate national festivals.

Fareiba does not want to return to Afghanistan because the situation remains dangerous. She is now doing well at school and hopes to get good grades. When she grows up, she hopes to be a doctor.

Muhammad's Story

Muhammad comes from a village in Afghanistan. In the 1990s, after the communist government collapsed, there was civil war in his country. Then the Taliban gained power in the mid-1990s. They persecuted Muhammad's community because they are Hazaras, an ethnic minority group. When Muhammad was six years old, his family escaped from Afghanistan.

During 1996 Taliban fighters came regularly to Muhammad's village. They seized men and took them away. His father, Sadiq, and the other men used to hide in the forest when they knew a Taliban raid was likely. It was stressful living in such a state of fear, so the family sold all their cows and sheep and left their land. They began the hazardous journey to neighboring Pakistan.

Traveling was hard because they had to go through Taliban-controlled territory. Hazaras look different from other Afghans so the Taliban could easily spot them. The Taliban are Pashtuns, so the family often paid Pashtuns to guide them through Taliban areas. They also had to bribe soldiers to let them through the checkpoints. There were other dangers too. Many people were robbed on their journey, or even killed.

▶ **A Hazara local leader digs up pieces of clothing from a mass grave in a village in Mazar-e Sharif in northern Afghanistan in 2002. The clothing belonged to people killed by the Taliban. The killings took place in August 1998, when the Taliban massacred large numbers of the population, especially Hazaras. It is thought that as many as 8,000 people were massacred in and around Mazar-e Sharif that summer.**

People smugglers

Many countries have introduced laws that make it hard for asylum seekers to enter legally. Some people, desperate to escape their country, turn to people smugglers. The smugglers charge their customers a high fee to sneak them illegally over an international border. Some refugees risk their entire life's savings on an uncertain journey that might lead to safety—but could lead to arrest and deportation back to their homeland.

It took Muhammad's family two days riding rickety buses on bumpy old roads to reach the Pakistani border. They did not have passports so they bribed the border guards to allow them to cross into Pakistan.

The family made their way to Quetta. Afghan refugees are allowed to work in Pakistan, but it is hard to find a job. The family made a living by making Afghan carpets. Like many Afghan children, Muhammad had to work as well as go to school. He found that the local people were friendly although the Pakistani police often harassed Afghan refugees.

Dreaming of a safer life for his family, Sadiq made the risky decision to pay a people smuggler to get him to Australia. The rest of the family did not know if he would survive the journey or if they would ever be reunited. The journey was long, dangerous, and expensive; the family had to sell their land in Afghanistan to pay the fee.

Sadiq traveled in a group of about ten people. The people smuggler organized passports and plane tickets for the group to fly to Indonesia. Then the group had to wait a couple of months before boarding a boat to take them to Australia. Muhammad's

► Hazara students at a school for Afghan refugees in Quetta, Pakistan. A major city near the Pakistan–Afghanistan border, Quetta has been a magnet for Afghan refugees since 1979, and there are large numbers of Hazaras there.

▶ Australian police scuffle with a group of people protesting against the detention of asylum seekers in Australia. The demonstration took place in front of the Baxter detention center in 2003. As well as protesting, supporters of refugees also visited and befriended them while they were in detention.

father said the boat was just 75 feet (23 meters, m) long and 26 feet (8 m) wide, and there were 230 people on board. They were terrified of falling in the water.

The boat landed on Ashmore Reef, an uninhabited island. Fortunately, the Australian Coast Guard spotted the refugees after one day and took them to Darwin in northern Australia.

Sadiq and the others were sent to Woomera detention center. At this time, all asylum seekers were detained until their claim had been assessed. Most people spent eight or nine months in detention. In a long interview, Sadiq had to explain his whole story before he was eventually granted a visa to stay in Australia. Many asylum seekers were not so lucky.

After obtaining his visa to live in Melbourne, Sadiq sponsored Muhammad, his brothers, sisters and mother, offering money and assistance so they could join him. They had been separated for five years. Life is better now that the family is together again.

Australia's detention policy

In 1992 the Australian government brought in new rules to deter asylum seekers. Those who arrived without correct travel documents were detained until a visa had been issued. If rejected, they were deported. Even families with young children were locked up. Refugees and their supporters protested vigorosly against the policy. In 2008 it was overturned. Asylum seekers were permitted to live in the community while their claim was being processed.

Aida's Story

Following World War II, Bosnia became a republic of communist Yugoslavia. In 1992, after the collapse of Yugoslavia, Bosnia declared its independence. The Serbian population of Bosnia objected, and war broke out between the country's Serbs, Croats, and Muslims. Aida lived through the war in the Bosnian capital, Sarajevo, where the fighting was intense. The war split up her family; some of them had to stay, while the pressure forced others to escape.

Aida was born and raised in Sarajevo—her family had lived there for many years. Her father is a doctor, her mother a nurse. When the war broke out, they felt it was their duty to stay and help save people's lives. Sarajevo was besieged, and it was too dangerous to go out. Aida spent much of the time in basements because of the shelling. She lost touch with her school friends and does not even know what happened to most of them.

During the war Aida's parents worked around the clock. They were continually exhausted from long hours of helping the injured. Young men were made to fight. Aida's 18-year-old brother was forced to join the army. Aida was always scared for her parents and brother. The situation grew even more frightening. She regularly saw people being killed and dead bodies on the streets. Aida will never forget those horrifying scenes.

Eventually, Aida's parents realized they could take no more. They wanted to leave. Aida's brother was not permitted to leave the army, however. Her sister had gotten married and decided to stay. So Aida fled with her parents.

The siege of Sarajevo

In April 1992 Bosnian Serb forces besieged Sarajevo. The city endured four years of continuous shelling and sniper attacks. It was reported that more than 10,000 people died, of whom 1,800 were children. Many buildings were destroyed or damaged. In 1995 NATO intervened, ordering the bombing of the Bosnian Serbs. This forced them to negotiate and end the siege.

The family went to Washington, DC. Aida found it hard to settle in at school at first. Even though she comes from a city, some teachers held stereotyped views about refugees. Once she was asked if she knew what a pen was! She had never felt so patronized in her life. Most people around her were kind though, and she gradually overcame the hurdles of a different language and culture. She believes it is extremely important for people to extend the hand of friendship to refugees. It makes so much difference to their lives.

▲ These refugee women and children are being evacuated from war-torn Sarajevo in 1992 and will be taken in by a European country. It is estimated that more than two million people were displaced during the 1992–95 Bosnian war. Between 1993 and 2003, 143,000 Bosnians were resettled in the United States.

Aida has great plans for the future. Her deepest desire is to be a singer—she has a lot to say and she loves singing. Just in case this doesn't work out, she hopes to go to college and study psychology. She would like to stay in the United States, which has become her home.

Marek's Story

The Roma were originally a traveling people from India. Today they form a significant minority in eastern European countries. They suffer discrimination at the hands of the majority population and their rights are not respected. Owing to this discrimination, the Roma generally live in poor conditions, have a low level of education and do the lowest-paid jobs. As a Roma family in the Czech Republic, Marek's family were repeatedly attacked until eventually they had no choice but to flee.

The Roma

The Roma are an ethnic group with their own language and culture. They left India around the tenth century CE and moved to different parts of the world. Today there are around ten million Roma in Europe, forming the largest ethnic minority on the continent. They mainly live in the Balkans and central and eastern Europe.

Marek was used to the verbal attacks. As a young man he'd be having a quiet drink with his friends and Czechs would start shouting, "Get out, you gypsies!"

▶ A little girl stands in a shabby courtyard in the Roma part of a town in North Bohemia in the Czech Republic. Many Roma in Czech cities live in poor conditions without basic services. They lack adequate sanitation and are not secure in their homes—landlords often evict them. Racial discrimination is a major problem. Czech officials do little to prevent this and in many cases they actively promote it.

▲ Far-right Workers' Party (DS) members hold an anti-Roma demonstration near a mainly Roma housing estate in Litvinov, Czech Republic, in 2008. The DS said it was campaigning "against positive discrimination" in the neighborhood. Yet far from experiencing special treatment from the government, the Roma live in poor conditions and have high unemployment levels.

The term *gypsies* was very insulting. If the police were called, they didn't help. They shouted at Marek and his friends too and sent them home.

One night, four young neo-Nazis viciously attacked Marek as he was leaving a disco. The neo-Nazis hate the Roma. They say they are not proper Czechs and do not belong in the Czech Republic. This group kicked Marek repeatedly and left him on the ground unconscious. A police patrol happened to drive past and saved his life. The attackers were caught but they were not given a prison sentence. The judge thought they would mend their ways. Yet they continued their neo-Nazi activities. Marek's mother Anna saw one of her son's attackers at a neo-Nazi demonstration a few years after the attack.

After the brutal attack, Marek's parents were so worried that they wanted him to leave the Czech Republic and live with relatives abroad. Marek did not agree. Four people had attacked him, not the whole country, so why should he quit his studies and home because of them?

The neo-Nazis in eastern Europe

Neo-Nazi groups are far-right organizations that want to restore Nazism. They believe in a pure nation made up only of white people from their country and aim to expel everyone else. Neo-Nazi groups are growing, particularly in eastern European countries, including Russia, Hungary, the Czech Republic, and Slovakia. They blame migrants and refugees for economic problems and carry out violent attacks against them.

The problems continued though. The attackers were supposed to pay compensation money to Marek because they had hurt him, but only two of them paid up. Some of their friends then beat up his father in revenge for taking the attackers to court. They forced him to return the money. Also, Marek's family noticed the neo-Nazis gathering support. They were marching through the streets, and the government did nothing to stop them.

Then Marek's sister was attacked. Five men and a woman cornered her and yelled racist abuse at her. The police arrived but they said there was nothing they could do—that's just how people are.

By now Marek's parents felt they simply did not have the strength to try to take his sister's attackers to court. Before Marek's attack, they believed it was possible to achieve justice through the courts. This time they realized that, as Roma, they would not be treated fairly.

Marek's mother Anna wanted the family to go as far away as possible. Terrified of neo-Nazis, they were eager to leave Europe where far-right parties are growing everywhere. They traveled across the Atlantic to Canada to claim asylum.

Moving was a huge sacrifice. All the family were working or studying in the Czech Republic and hated the idea of relying on welfare benefits in another country. Marek was in the middle of a college course, and his sister had just been accepted by a good university. But the family simply could not risk any further attacks.

Lamara's Story

Chechnya is a republic in southwestern Russia. In 1991, as the Soviet Union was collapsing, Chechnya declared itself independent. In 1994 Russia invaded to try to take control again, leading to a long and bloody conflict that has devastated the republic. It is estimated that up to 250,000 people were killed and more than 400,000 were forced to leave their homes during the 1990s. The war continued in the 2000s. During the conflict, Lamara watched while her mother and father were attacked in their own home.

Lamara's family lived through two wars in the capital Grozny—first when the Russians attacked in 1994, and then when fighting broke out again in 1999. Even after the later attacks, the conflict continued. Armed groups used to break into homes at night and kidnap people. One night armed men burst into Lamara's apartment and beat up her parents.

▲ In Grozny, 2001, soldiers from the pro-Russian Chechen special militia forces combat the Chechens fighting for independence from Russia. They search for ambushes and mines on the road. Russian troops returned to Chechnya in 1999, leading to a period of intensive conflict with Chechen fighters.

Chechnya—the economic issues

Chechnya is important economically. It is located near the huge oilfields of the Caspian Sea. An oil pipeline runs through Chechnya, and petroleum refineries are concentrated in Grozny. The region also has natural gas supplies. After Chechnya became independent, Russia lost control of these resources. The desire to bring them back under Russian authority was an important reason for the invasion. However, the long war in Chechnya destroyed the economy.

Her parents made a quick decision to seek asylum in Belgium, where they had heard there was good medical care. Lamara's mother Amina needed surgery and Lamara required counseling after the terrible trauma of witnessing the attack. Her parents knew a man who had contacts in the countries on the way to Belgium. The family had to pay a huge amount of money to people smugglers to buy passports and take them to Belgium. They were fearful about leaving their homeland and felt uncertain about the long and risky journey.

▲ It is common for refugees to hide in trucks heading for their target country. In 2009 hundreds of migrants camped in woods near Calais, northern France. The area was known locally as the "jungle." Each night they tried to board trucks about to cross by train or ferry to the UK. In September 2009 the French police destroyed the settlement but the refugees remained determined to reach Britain.

▶ Chechen children at a refugee center in Poland, September 2004. Earlier that month, militants fighting for Chechen independence took more than 1,000 people hostage in a school in Beslan, southern Russia. During fighting between the militants and Russian security forces, over 300 people were killed, including 186 children. Afterwards, the number of Chechens seeking refuge in Poland increased.

The family successfully crossed the eastern Polish border and their passports were stamped. In Poland they had to climb into a truck loaded with furniture to go to Germany, then on to Belgium. It was horrible in the truck. It was freezing cold, and they had to sleep on the bare, hard floor. Once in Belgium they took the train to the capital, Brussels. It was luxury after the misery of the truck. The whole journey from Grozny took 12 days.

Lamara's family went straight to the Belgian Aliens Office (department for foreigners) to claim asylum. They had to wait six months to find out if they would be accepted. It was a difficult time—they couldn't settle because they had no idea if they would be allowed to stay or not. Luckily, Amina was able to have the surgery she needed, but Lamara did not get the counseling she had hoped for.

After the long wait, the family were told they had been refused asylum because of the stamp in their passports from the Polish authorities. The officials said that Poland should accept them because they had arrived there first. Lamara's family was hugely disappointed; their hazardous journey had proved pointless. They were sent to a deportation camp, and Lamara became ill while they were there. Her bad health meant they could not be deported for several months. Finally, the family was sent back. After the long, arduous and costly journey to Brussels, it took just two hours to return to Poland.

After a while, Lamara's family accepted that Poland would be their home and became used to life there. Lamara received the psychological counseling she so desperately needed, and she and her sister started school. Her mother is taking hairdressing and cookery classes. She says that if she had known how terrible the experience of seeking asylum would be, she would never have considered leaving Chechnya. Yet the family had lost their sense of security there. They are working to regain this in Poland, but do not yet feel secure.

Aguek's Story

Between 1983 and 2005, civil war raged in Sudan as government forces fought the Sudan People's Liberation Army (SPLA). The government sent an Arab military force to fight against its rivals in southern Sudan, mainly the Dinka people. Aguek was a Dinka and one of thousands of children who lost contact with their parents or were orphaned during the war and fled Sudan. They became known as the "Lost Children of Sudan."

Aguek's village was attacked by government troops in 1987. Together with other boys and girls, he walked barefoot across southern Sudan to an Ethiopian refugee camp. In the camp the children attended lessons in the open air. At first Aguek was not interested, but then he heard that the teachers were giving out cookies at the end of class. He started going to school. Four years later the camp was attacked by Ethiopian troops. Along with many others, Aguek was chased back to Sudan. The survivors walked hundreds of miles to Kenya. Large numbers died on the journey but Aguek survived and reached Kakuma refugee camp.

Now a teenager, Aguek returned to school, where he excelled and was offered a scholarship to attend a Kenyan boarding school. There were no luxuries there—food was as scarce as in the refugee camp, but the educational standard was high. A top student, Aguek was fortunate enough to be accepted, along with around 3,800 other "Lost Children," for resettlement in the United States.

The "Lost Children of Sudan"

More than 20,000 Sudanese children were separated from their families after their villages were attacked. They walked in large groups to Ethiopia—the journey took three months. Large numbers starved to death or were killed by wild animals. Four years later civil war broke out in Ethiopia, and they fled back to Sudan. Many drowned crossing the Gilo River or were eaten by crocodiles. The survivors remained for about 18 months in Sudan before walking to Kakuma camp in Kenya. In all they walked about 1,000 miles (1,600 kilometers, km).

He arrived in Burlington, Vermont, in 2001, eager to continue his education. The refugees needed a high school diploma to take an English-language test and had to pay their own living expenses. Already in possession of a high school diploma, Aguek took a job stacking shelves in a Sears store. Within a year of arriving in Burlington he got into the University of Vermont and graduated three-and-a-half years later in economics. He won awards for his academic achievements.

▲ Some of a group of around 3,500 "Lost Children" returning from Itang refugee camp in Ethiopia to Nasir in southern Sudan in 2002. It was extremely hard for the children to get an education in refugee camps. Textbooks and paper were scarce; many children learned to read and write by drawing with their fingers in the sand. They were often hungry, which made it difficult to concentrate on their studies.

After graduation, Aguek flew back to Kenya to marry a Dinka woman, also a refugee. He managed to make contact with his parents, who traveled from Sudan for the wedding and an emotional reunion. It was the first time they had seen each other in 18 years. Aguek returned to Burlington, where his wife soon joined him and started college. He took up a post at the University of Vermont while continuing his studies. As Aguek says, "Education is our mother and father." He would not have survived without it.

Jonathan's Story

Eritrea fought a long war against Ethiopia to win independence, which was eventually granted in 1993. However, there were still points of conflict between the two countries, which led to a further war between 1998 and 2000. Tens of thousands of people died. Jonathan grew up in the north of Eritrea during wartime. He could not join the army because of his faith and was punished for this.

Certain minority Christian groups, including Jehovah's Witnesses, are persecuted in Eritrea. Sometimes the police interrupt them while they are worshipping at home, take them away and beat them. For this reason, when soldiers burst into his home, Jonathan knew he was in trouble. Firstly, it is compulsory to enlist in the army in Eritrea, especially during wartime. He was only 16 years old but because he was overweight he looked older. Also, Jonathan is a Jehovah's Witness. His religion does not permit him to take up arms.

In the vain hope he might avoid army duty, Jonathan showed the soldiers his identity card, proving his religion, but they ignored it and dragged him off to prison. There he was badly beaten and suffered psychological torture. Soldiers would take away one of his cell mates. Shortly afterwards Jonathan would hear the sound of a single gunshot, and the soldiers told him the man had been shot dead. This happened several times. Sometimes Jonathan thought this was a trick to frighten him and force him to join the army, but he never saw those cell mates again.

After a month, Jonathan was freed at dawn and taken to his grandfather's house. Two weeks later the soldiers returned to enlist him, but he had slipped away to his uncle's house. He took heed of the warning and fled the country for Egypt, where he stayed for three months on a tourist visa. Before the visa expired, he bought a ticket for Honduras. From there he traveled to Europe to meet his father, who had US citizenship. He first arrived in Barcelona, Spain, and then went to Madrid. Insisting he could not return to Eritrea, he claimed asylum.

Jonathan was fortunate; his asylum claim was successful. He found a job as a librarian for Spanish TV.

Child soldiers in Africa

At any one time, around 300,000 children are fighting in armed groups worldwide. The problem is worst in Africa. Most child soldiers are aged between 15 and 18 but there are some as young as seven. They are often seized from their homes or schools and forced to join up. Some join to earn some money because their family is desperately poor. Others have been orphaned and have no other chance to make a living. Children are recruited not only to fight but also to provide services to the armed forces, working as scouts, porters, cooks, spies or sex slaves.

▲ An Ethiopian boy soldier in Addis Ababa. In 2001 the Coalition to Stop the Use of Child Soldiers reported that Ethiopia had forced thousands of secondary school students to fight as soldiers in the 1998–2000 war with Eritrea. A UNHCR report from the same year indicated that Eritrea had also used child soldiers.

Faisal's Story

Since the 1990s there has been civil war in Uganda between the government and rebel forces, particularly the Lord's Resistance Army (LRA). The LRA kidnapped thousands of children, forcing them to fight the government, and carried out brutal attacks on civilians. The conflict has displaced more than a million people. Faisal's father was threatened by both the government and rebel forces. He disappeared, and none of the family knew if he was dead or alive. Faisal, his mother and brother fled in fear and sought asylum in the UK.

The family settled near Glasgow in Scotland while they were waiting for their asylum claim to be processed. Faisal's mother became involved in helping other asylum seekers

and protesting against their unfair treatment. Four years later, Faisal was 12 and happily settled at school.

One day after school the whole family was called to the immigration center. Thinking it was a routine trip, they were shocked to find they were being arrested. The immigration office had decided that the family had no right to asylum and wanted to arrest them in case they went into hiding. Faisal's mother asked for permission to call a lawyer but her request was refused.

The two boys, still in their school uniforms, were sent immediately with their mother to Dungavel detention center. This is a prison where asylum seekers are held until they are

◀ **Children sleeping in a shelter built by a Christian charity in northern Uganda, 2004. Shelters like this one protect children from being kidnapped by the LRA. The children go to the shelters before nightfall and return home in the morning.**

▲ These small children are at a 2005 protest by supporters of asylum seekers outside Dungavel detention center. Campaigners were particularly concerned because entire families were kept in detention at the facility. They called for the asylum seekers to be housed in open, hotel-like accommodation.

deported. Subsequently they were moved to Yarl's Wood in England, a deliberate move to keep them away from their community and make it harder for their friends to protest against their detention.

Being in Yarl's Wood was extremely traumatic for Faisal and his little brother. They were locked in a cell in a prison surrounded by guards, high fences and barbed wire. They were terrified of being sent back to Uganda, where Faisal's mother could face death.

Fortunately, the family's supporters stood by them. Fearing their friends were about to be deported, they hired a van and drove about 375 miles (600 km) from Glasgow to Yarl's Wood. They held a protest outside the detention center. About 70 people demonstrated in Glasgow the following weekend.

A couple of weeks later, the deportation order was canceled, and the family was allowed to return home. They had to fight for the right to remain indefinitely in the UK, and eventually succeeded. Faisal's mother continues to assist asylum seekers.

The detention of asylum seekers

Many countries detain some asylum seekers. For example, the US government places asylum seekers in detention if it believes they entered the country illegally. The UK government detains asylum seekers it considers are dangerous or may attempt to evade deportation. Australia used to lock up all asylum seekers but the law changed in 2008 (see page 21). Supporters of asylum seekers say it is wrong to imprison asylum seekers as if they were criminals.

Flores's Story

Between 1998 and 2003 a devastating civil war in the Democratic Republic of Congo (DRC) killed around four million people. During the war the DRC government was supported by several African countries: Angola, Chad, Namibia, Sudan, and Zimbabwe. The rebel forces had the backing of Uganda and Rwanda. The DRC is rich in natural resources, including gold, diamonds and coltan (see panel). All the parties in the war were accused of becoming involved in order to gain a share of these resources.

When Flores Sukula was 15, her mother was beaten and threatened, so the family fled the DRC. Flores's father had already gone into hiding because he was suspected of being an opponent of the government. Then government soldiers attacked her mother in front of the four children. They said they would return and kill the entire family if they failed to reveal the whereabouts of Flores's father.

The Sukula family escaped to the UK and claimed asylum. The immigration officials dealing with the case said that Flores's mother was lying and that her claim was unfounded. The family's welfare benefits were taken away, and since asylum seekers are not allowed to work, they had to rely on charity to survive. They depended on donations, even for diapers and milk for the youngest member of the family.

Then the Sukulas received a letter saying that they might be thrown out of their home. They discovered that the government had the right to take the children away from their mother because she was now too poor to look after them. Flores's mother became extremely depressed. Flores's seven-year-old brother suffered from stress and found it hard to cope at school.

Flores, now 19, was studying to be a midwife. Her 15-year-old brother was in school studying for important exams. Despite their commitments, the pair decided they had to set up an anti-deportation campaign. They made public speeches and wrote

The DRC and coltan

The struggle over access to the mineral coltan has fuelled the bitter conflict in eastern DRC. Coltan is an ore used in electronic devices such as mobile phones and laptops. From 1999, as the market for these goods rapidly increased, the price of coltan rose dramatically. Rebel forces, as well as Rwandan and Ugandan military forces, moved into the region to extract coltan and profit from the trade. A UN report has shown that many Western corporations were financing the rebel groups to gain access to coltan and thus contributed to the expansion of the conflict.

▲ 2003: an armed soldier from a rebel group, the Union of Congolese Patriots, stands on guard during a rally by his leader, Thomas Lubanga, in Ituri, eastern DRC. Violence between the Hema and Lendu peoples, and between militia groups vying for control over mines, claimed tens of thousands of lives from 1999 to 2009. In 2009 Lubanga was put on trial by the International Criminal Court for war crimes.

letters explaining why they were terrified of being returned to the DRC. Flores even addressed a meeting in parliament. The family gained the support of the local newspaper and several trade unions. Local social workers said they would refuse to take the children away from their mother.

When the authorities at Flores's school threatened to expel her as a failed asylum seeker, the students and teachers campaigned to prevent that from happening.

▲ Thousands of protesters demonstrate against the French government's immigration policy in Paris in 2008. They called on the government to make all immigrants legal. The demonstration was held a day after a 29-year-old man from Mali died after jumping into the Marne River as he was escaping from the police. The banner reads: "Regularization of all the illegal immigrants. No raids, no deportation, no exploitation."

Anti-deportation campaigns

Campaigns against deportation organize to oppose laws that make it hard for refugees to seek asylum. They also support individuals who are threatened with deportation. Members of the campaign seek support from the schools and workplaces of the threatened individuals, from local community organizations, government officials and trade unions. They hold public meetings and protests and contact the media to raise the profile of the campaign. In some cases a small group of dedicated people succeed in preventing a deportation.

The campaigners said that if the authorities tried to force the Sukulas out of their home, they would make a physical blockade around the house to stop them. The campaign worked and the local council agreed that it would not evict them.

The family had to endure 17 months of relying on community support and funds from the defense campaign. In the end, thanks to the efforts of the family and all their supporters, they won the right to remain in the UK.

Samira's Story

Somalia has suffered from civil war since 1991 when the groups that overthrew the existing government began to fight among themselves. In 2000 a new government was formed but was unable to control the country. Six years later an Islamic party took over a large area of southern Somalia. The government resisted, with support from Ethiopia. The renewed fighting caused a new wave of refugees. Overall, hundreds of thousands of Somalis have been forced to flee the horrors of war, mostly seeking safety in neighboring lands.

▲ A local woman stands among ruined buildings in Mogadishu, the capital of Somalia, in 1992. The city suffered widespread devastation during the civil war of the 1990s. Violence continued periodically in the early 2000s. Fighting in Mogadishu was renewed in 2007 and 2008 as Somali groups fought each other and struggled against the Ethiopian and international peacekeeping forces. A large proportion of the city's residents were forced to flee.

Dadaab

Run by UNHCR with the assistance of other refugee agencies, Dadaab is a series of three huge refugee camps in Kenya, established to offer shelter to Somalis who fled during the crisis of 1991. The vast majority of refugees in the camps are Somali, although some are from Sudan, Uganda, DRC and other war-torn countries. Some refugees have lived in Dadaab for more than ten years. Originally built for 90,000 refugees, the camps now house three times that number. It is a challenge to provide enough land, water, and waste disposal for everyone and to educate all the children.

The war in Somalia had devastating consequences for Samira's family. In 2005, when she was 14, her Hungarian father and three siblings were killed when gunmen attacked their home. Her mother and the four youngest children fled. Samira was at school when this happened, so her life was saved. She waited three years in her home for the rest of the family to return. A neighbor took care of her and she continued to attend school. Her family did not return, and Samira started to give up hope that she would ever see them again.

Eventually, Samira's carer advised her to leave Somalia and seek refuge in Dadaab camp in Kenya. Now 18, she left everything behind and traveled there alone. Dadaab was a shock to her. It was an enormous camp with a total population of 280,000 refugees. She had assistance from the international refugee agency, the United Nations High Commissioner for Refugees (UNHCR), but nevertheless she had to live and survive alone.

Samira had always tended to attract attention because of her looks. She has light skin because of her Hungarian father. When she was living with her family and had their support, she could cope with being different. But now she decided not to go to school because she was scared of being teased. When a UNHCR worker discovered her absence, Samira explained her situation. Fortunately she had documents from her dead father that proved he was Hungarian. When she showed the evidence to UNHCR workers, they realized that Samira was probably entitled to Hungarian citizenship. They contacted the Hungarian authorities in Budapest, who confirmed that this was the case. Samira was offered the possibility to leave Africa and start a new life in a country she had never visited.

Events took a rapid turn. An older man, who had heard about Samira's situation, tried to persuade her to marry him in the hope that he would be able to travel to Europe with her. Samira needed to leave immediately to break away from him. Hungarian Baptist Aid, a Christian charity, put Samira on a plane to Nairobi. At the Hungarian embassy she was given travel documents to allow her to travel to Europe.

When Samira arrived in Hungary, the local authorities informed her that her 19-year-old brother Sándor was also in Hungary. He had arrived in Hungary a few months earlier with some other Somali asylum seekers. Amazed and delighted, Samira was soon reunited with Sándor after seven years apart. Hungarian Baptist Aid helped the pair to get in touch with their father's brother and sister, who welcomed them into their home. Their case attracted so much attention in both Kenya and Hungary that it enabled Samira to locate the rest of the family. She discovered that her mother and four little brothers and sisters were living near Mogadishu in Somalia. Another brother was found in Dadaab.

Samira and Sándor gained official recognition as Hungarian citizens and hoped the rest of the family could join them. Unfortunately her mother and younger siblings were not able to get visas to come to Hungary. Yet at least Samira knows that most of her family are alive and she no longer feels alone in the world.

▲ **These Somali children attend an outdoor class at Dagahaley refugee camp, part of Dadaab, in June 2009. They are part of a wave of tens of thousands of people who were forced to leave their homes due to intense fighting in Somalia. The overcrowded conditions in Dadaab allowed an outbreak of measles to spread, and there were tensions with the local community over access to pasture and water.**

Emily and Breyen's Story

Robert Mugabe has ruled Zimbabwe since 1980. In 2008 the results of the country's presidential election were disputed. Mugabe clung on to power, although many believed he had lost the election to his opponent, Morgan Tsvangirai. The political crisis came on top of severe economic and social problems—high unemployment and a massive decline in health and welfare conditions. Emily and Breyen, 22-year-old cousins, were desperate to escape poverty and persecution.

Robert Mugabe

In 1987 President Mugabe turned Zimbabwe from a parliamentary democracy into a one-party state. During the 1990s he faced growing unrest because of economic problems and opposition to his rule. In 1999 the Movement for Democratic Change (MDC), led by Morgan Tsvangirai, was formed to oppose Mugabe. The president's supporters used violence and intimidation against the MDC to ensure that it did not win the elections in 2000, 2002 or 2005. However, after the disputed 2008 elections, Mugabe and Tsvangirai reached a power-sharing agreement. Yet there were doubts that Mugabe would relinquish any power.

The young women hoped to find safety in South Africa. Some men offered to help them cross the border. They turned out to be people smugglers, who took all their money and brought them to Musina, just over the border in South Africa.

The cousins soon realized how lucky they had been. Other young women had been beaten and raped by their escorts after being robbed. A kind gas station attendant advised them to go to a church-run women's shelter. They stayed here while making their asylum claim. They received a permit allowing them to remain in South Africa until their claim was decided.

Now the cousins are looking for a job. If the situation improves in Zimbabwe, they will return.

◄ Thousands of refugees, mainly Zimbabweans, wait to enter a refugee centre in Johannesburg, South Africa, in 2008. Some were met with kindness, but that year Johannesburg witnessed a wave of attacks on Zimbabweans.

Paula's Story

Paula is from Colombia, South America. She now lives in the United States with her mother, brother and sister. Her father was a sergeant in the Colombian army. In Colombia there is fighting between the army and the guerrilla groups that oppose the government. One of these groups captured her father and sentenced him to death. They attacked him and threw him in a river to drown.

The following week Paula's mother Diana found out that her husband had been killed. Then she received death threats. Terrified, the family fled to another part of the country. Diana remarried. Yet the family continued to receive threats, so they had to keep moving. Finally, they left Colombia altogether. They traveled to Quito, the capital of Ecuador, and applied for asylum in the United States.

▲ Two girls in traditional dresses hold Guatemalan flags at a Central American parade in Chicago. Like Colombians, many Guatemalans have been forced to flee their country because of armed conflict.

After being interviewed by US officials, Paula's family was permitted to move to the United States. Diana's new husband could not come because his claim had not yet been accepted, but they hoped he would be able to join them soon.

The Methodist Christian congregation in Dallas, Texas, sponsored Paula's family so they were able to settle there. She and her brother and sister started school. They still feel shocked from their experiences and Paula worries about her stepdad. However, the family are gradually starting to lose their fears and adapt to their new life.

Glossary

asylum seeker A refugee who claims the right to live in safety in another country because of persecution in his or her own country.

besiege Surround an enemy city with soldiers so that people cannot enter or leave.

checkpoint A place, often on a border between two countries, where people have to stop to have their documents checked.

citizenship The legal right to belong to a particular country.

civil war A war between groups of people within the same country.

communist Describing a political system in which the government controls the production of goods and the running of services.

deportation Forcing a person to leave a country.

detention center A secure place, like a prison.

discrimination Treating a group of people worse than others because of a difference in, for example, skin colour, culture or religion.

displaced Forced to leave home and move to another part of the country.

embassy The place of work for officials who represent their government in another country.

ethnic minority A group of people who have a different culture, religion, language or skin colour from most other people in their society.

guerrilla group A group of irregular (non-government) soldiers who fight a regular army, usually with the aim of overthrowing the government.

immigration A permanent move to another country.

internally displaced person (IDP) Someone who has been forced to leave their home and move to a different part of the country.

migrant Someone who moves from one part of a country to another, or to another country.

neo-Nazi People today who believe in the supremacy of white people and are racist towards nonwhite people.

occupation Moving into another country and taking control of it by military force.

one-party state A system of government in which only one political party is allowed.

parliament An assembly of elected representatives that governs a nation.

parliamentary democracy A system of government in which voters elect people to represent them in parliament.

Pashtun The Pashto-speaking people of southeastern Afghanistan and northwestern Pakistan.

people smuggler A person who arranges for people to travel illegally to another country.

persecution Treating people badly because of their ethnic group or culture, or because of their religious or political beliefs.

refugee A person who has been forced to leave his or her own country because it is too dangerous to stay there.

refugee camp A camp built by governments or international organizations to shelter large numbers of refugees.

resettlement Being settled in a new country.

shelling The firing of shells – metal cases filled with explosives – from large guns.

sniper Someone who shoots at people from a hidden position.

social worker Someone who is paid to give help and advice to people who have problems.

sponsor A person who supports someone else, for example when they move to another country, by helping to pay for his or her needs.

stereotype Negative ideas about a whole group of people, which are not based on facts.

Taliban A strict Islamic group that took control of most of Afghanistan between 1996 and 2001.

trade union An organization of workers that exists to protect its members' interests and improve their working conditions.

visa A mark in a passport that gives its holder permission to enter a country.

welfare benefits Practical help, such as money or services, given to needy people.

Further Information

Books

Bradman, Tony. *Give Me Shelter: An Asylum Seeker Anthology*. Frances Lincoln Publishers, 2007.

Dalton, Dave. *People on the Move: Refugees and Asylum Seekers*. Heinemann, 2006.

Naidoo, Beverley. *The Other Side of Truth*. Puffin, 2007.

Senker, Cath. *Global Questions: Why Do People Seek Asylum?* Franklin Watts, 2008.

Senker, Cath. *The Global Village: Migration and Refugees*. Evans Brothers Ltd, 2008.

Zephaniah, Benjamin. *Refugee Boy*. A&C Black, 2008.

Resource for teachers

Rutter, Jill. *Refugees: We Left Because We Had To*. Refugee Council, 2004.

Websites

www.itvs.org/beyondthefire

Beyond the Fire: teenage experiences of war and life as refugees in the United States.

www.irespect.net/True%20Storie

iRespect: a collection of true stories about child refugees and asylum seekers in the UK.

www.refugeecouncil.org.uk/practice/basics

Refugee Council, UK: links to basic information about asylum, refugees and other resources.

news.bbc.co.uk/hi/english/static/in_depth/world/2001/road_to_refuge

The Road to Refuge: refugees tell the stories of their journey to safety.

Index